I0816152

SONG OF GRAY

THE COLORADO PRIZE FOR POETRY

ASHA FUTTERMAN

SONG OF GRAY

POEMS

The Center for Literary Publishing
Colorado State University

For information about permission to reproduce
selections from this book, write to
The Center for Literary Publishing
attn: Permissions
9105 Campus Delivery
Colorado State University
Fort Collins, Colorado 80523-9105.

Printed in the United States of America.

Library of Congress Cataloging-in-Publication Data

Names: Futterman, Asha, author.
Title: Song of gray : poems / Asha Futterman.
Description: Fort Collins, Colorado : The Center for Literary Publishing, Colorado State University, [2025]
Identifiers: LCCN 2025032350 (print) | LCCN 2025032351 (ebook) | ISBN 9781885635952 (paperback) | ISBN 9781885635969 (ebook)
Subjects: LCGFT: Poetry.
Classification: LCC PS3606.U8835 S56 2025 (print) | LCC PS3606.U8835 (ebook)
LC record available at https://lccn.loc.gov/2025032350
LC ebook record available at https://lccn.loc.gov/2025032351

The paper used in this book meets the minimum requirements of the American National Standard for Information Sciences-Permanence of Paper for Printed Library Materials, ANSI Z39.48-1984.

For Kenny Tatum

I shall not sing a May song.
A May song should be gay.
I'll wait until November.
And sing a song of gray.

—Gwendolyn Brooks

contents

i

ii

iii

*

it's nice to take drugs and sit in the hot tub but first you have to find your suit

I walk around
looking for my locker
while the naked women
discuss swimming pools
at different YMCAs
Kirkwood is a no
Brentwood is okay
but Carondelet
Carondelet is beautiful
you can see
the sun setting
from the pool
and nothing outside
can see you

when I met my boyfriend's
dad he told me a story
about one of his students
Devin has a problem:
Someone called Devin a nigger
and he smashed their windows
would you ever do
something like that
I tell him *I'm not sure*
but I know I wouldn't
when I look through

the window
I try to see the sky
but instead I see my face
when the naked ladies
look at me
they see nature
when I'm called a nigger
I'd like to know
the right way to look

I'm covered
in guilt
what are you
looking for
the naked ladies
ask me
after I've passed them
six or seven times
all of my things I say
they might be
behind you

incident report

I spent a few hours helping my friend
cut down a tree in his front yard and drag
its branches to the back
it was supposed to be a peach tree
but the peaches never grew

the neighbors call the city on him
to report the empty and overgrown branches
one night we burned them
and a neighbor came up to the fence

she said *it's not okay what you are doing*
those go in the green waste bin

it's fine I tell her   *I know how to use a tree*

performing

Chaclyn never locked
her bike
or the door to her house
she wanted to act
like she was living
in the world
she desires
a world without locks

I am an actor
but I don't act to live
in the world I desire
there are easier things
I could do

my boyfriend
is slow-moving
and neat

he tells me
if you wake up
and you're not in a rush
maybe make your bed

if you get home
and you're not in a rush

maybe take some of the trash
out of your car

I want to believe
in a difference

between myself
and my clown face

I perform
on Portland Place
I sing and dance
in front of the home
of an alt-right politician

there are two cop cars
guarding the audience
which includes
26 surgeons
several goldendoodles

when the show is over
I drive home
in a clean car

is this what acting
is good for

mastery

I auditioned to be a White woman
        I forgot a line
because I forgot my character
        was in a room with a window

I was in a room
        that was all mirrors

I think the best acting advice
        I ever got was to take off my shoes
and feel my feet on the ground

my acting teacher said
        it's easier to enter
an imagined reality
        when you are present
in the space

an anonymous blogger wrote
        There is also no place of the slave
The slave's reference to his or her quarters
        as home does not change the fact
that it is a spatial extension
        of the master's dominion

maybe I'm a bad actor
          because I'm unable to convince myself
of any sort of spatial belonging

or maybe I'm a good actor
          when I feel my feet
I feel my own transience

I keep the window open
          in my room at night
every 4am there's a dog
          that screams ambulances
that get closer
          then further away
or maybe only get further away

this year and every year

I am Midwestern Black and living in New York
the red clouds are shaped like rivers I saw the blood
in my mind in the clouds
each bird seems like it will fly into my face
before it flies to the ground to get crumbs
I can't think beyond the concrete
so I feel a little bit stupid
a man walks towards me
holding a stick I do not like to see
the desperation I feel

repetition

I give a poem to a poet
she wants to see it better
the woman she wants to see is dead
I don't want to bring her back to life
to see the desperation on her face before she died
I saw the man who killed her in a TV interview
he looked like he didn't talk to many people
the look on his face was
I don't really know how to describe it

I have seen the image
of the dead woman's face over and over
not her face but I have seen it
we have all seen seen it

my neighbor puts three orange cones
in front of his house every day
to save his favorite parking space
he watches *Two Broke Girls* in the backyard
he says his favorite lines aloud with the characters
same pauses same inflections
I can hear him from my sunroom

his mother never leaves the house
sometimes I see her sitting in her sunroom
from my sunroom

mastery

I used to idealize freedom until I read
that freedom doesn't exist without
slavery freedom is a concept
people made up to make slaves
work harder because they feel
there is something to work towards

freedom is idealized in all art
especially in contemporary theatre
where boys flail their limbs around
so honestly I cry and cry I feel silly
because I need form
to mimic any sort of freedom

the Suzuki method is a strict form
of acting that asks the actor to forget
they have a face and instead remember
that there is a warm light emanating
from the center of their flesh

to be a good Suzuki actor
one whose voice and body
can enter every audience member
the actor does not speak to the audience
instead they send their voice to the priest
who sits in the center of the theatre

and who is a conduit to the gods
then the gods decide
if the actor's voice is worth hearing

if so the gods send the actor's voice
back down to the priest and through the priest
the actor's voice pours out to the souls
of each audience member equally

once I did it I think
one time the gods decided
to send my voice back to earth
my acting teacher heard it
she asked the class
did you hear that

i am the machine and i work

my job used to be teaching a machine
to recognize complaints filed against police officers
that contained allegations of sexual violence
it wasn't very hard
all I had to do was read a lot of complaints
and tell the machine words
that were commonly used in the ones that alleged sexual violence
it didn't work though
it could never find anything I hadn't already found
the person I was working for told me and my coworkers
to read more complaints and give the machine more words
but there are only so many words
at a protest in the summer of 2020
she told a crowd of people to be quiet and lie down for 8 minutes
I just did it but one person awoke from her fake death and yelled
I am sick of lying on the street
nonsense is violence
it's also the view through my window
which is always cracked open
my neighbor sometimes sings
it's bad but not annoying
he doesn't mean for anyone to hear him

broken lyre

my hands are still my hands
like my grandfather's hands
are his hands and they
are on the window
attached to the body
of a cabbage white
and in the casket
attached to a face
that isn't his face

he died shoveling snow
that melted the next day
poetry makes nothing
happen

empathy

my favorite place
          was destroyed by Barack Obama
he's building a library
          in my neighborhood in the grass
where I liked to sit
          and watch my dogs play
I would have protested
          but the grass didn't have a name
it was in the shape of a circle though
          so I called it the circle garden
now it's called the Obama Center
          they always need to give a field
a body and a face
          so they can empathize with it
don't you think that's dangerous
          don't you think it's dangerous
to be naked where someone could see you
          I ask Arman while he pees in the woods
Arman says maybe
          communities should be three hundred people
we can give three hundred people
          a name and an argument
so if we don't want anyone
          in our community to be disposable
we should live in a place that small
          but I like Chicago

I want a neighborhood with everything
    the construction crew found a noose
on the site of the Obama Center
    I Google Image searched
and someone took a photo
    that zooms in on an almost clear plastic bag
with a noose in it
    the construction company is Black-owned
and offered $100,000 to anyone
    with information about the incident
there are some things
    we will never understand about each other
I would never let the trees see my body
    I tell Arman
it might give them pleasure

i feel connected to myself

when I think there is a guy watching me
    when I was younger
he was Robert Pattinson
    now he is more amorphous
sometimes a podcast host

other days a mousy girl a few days ago
    I saw their body
while I was taking a green bath

I should know the flesh
    I should know the flesh absent of self
I should know that one is real
    that one is imagined
I should know that
    one is black that one is green

my hair is suspended in webs around my house
    I notice a collection of little ones
under my altar
    after the voice of a real person
tells me to get on the ground

I do this every morning I stretch
    and then I try to understand
what is coming out of me

audition

the auditors
will tell you the risk
is story
and character
but they are wrong
the risk is what you look like
and your personality
I told a story
I was on my knees
in the center
of a white room
with a big table
behind which sat
more than one bald man
they told me to sing
and I sang
about the country
they told me to sing differently
so I looked out the window
and sang
to the pigeon
the auditor
said *thank you*
then told his colleagues
that I'm too afraid
of what's fake

to express
anything real
on Valentine's Day
I got an email
that said
I didn't get in
to theatre school
I called my boyfriend
to let him know
he said
I think
you're perfect
that notion
that notion
really resonates with me

how to be a contemporary performer

I was in Croatia
to learn how to be
a contemporary performer
for the first three days of learning
I slept in a room
with four boys
I felt my bed shift
when the boy above me
twitched in his sleep
that's good material
my performance teacher said
she likes my movements
but she's worried
I am exposing myself
she asks me
do you have shorts
for under those shorts
I don't
I don't have pants
anymore either
because I hung them
out to dry
and they blew
into someone else's lawn
the people who live
there didn't answer
the door when I knocked

when you are Black
nothing is secret
the lady who owns
the theatre yelled at me
for using the bathroom
you are not allowed
to do that
she yelled
my performance teacher likes
how I can
stand on one leg
longer than everyone
else in the class
the Finnish guy
in the program
went to use the bathroom
and the lady
who owns the theatre
was nice about it
I like him a lot
but he doesn't
even know how
to get out of a chair
without leaning forward
he keeps on forgetting
where his stomach is
which is the center

of everything
my body works

I want to tell
the lady who owns
the theatre *my body*
works even better
than yours

my type

when I had an agent
my agent told me
if I want parts
I need to figure out my type

your type is not
she offered
being from
a Black neighborhood

I got catcalled
the other day
but maybe it doesn't count

he yelled
can I get some of that hair?

at first I thought he said ass
but after a second I realized
he was bald

and wanted hair

I auditioned to be an understudy
in a play about slavery
and the slaves
have modern-day equivalents

as feuding college professors

I wanted to be in the play
    more than anything
but I didn't get it

    my mom said
it was probably because
    I don't have
a convincing slave voice

    don't worry

I should have told my agent

    my type is out there
calling for me

measure your savings

I walk to the grocery store today my favorite is Ruler Foods because I would like to measure my savings

sometimes I measure how much time I spend on my right foot and how much time I spend on my left and I asked Dr. Drew to measure how much of a narcissist I am he said my vanity level is medium my superiority level is medium and all the other levels are low which I thought was pretty good but still a little embarrassing

I want to make latkes there are no organic eggs at Ruler *hello excuse me where are the organic eggs there are no organic eggs but look at these eggs they are free-range and they are brown and they taste the same* I don't know what an egg tastes like

but wolves at the wolf sanctuary do Angela says they eat the eggs whole shell and all she likes the wolf sanctuary but they force the wolves to have sex with each other and say it's for their own good the workers even make up little love stories to make themselves feel better about it   I would never work there   or at Ruler Foods I work at a bar that serves humans and dogs instead called BarK which is pronounced Bar Kay

Angela works at the bougiest grocery store in St. Louis it's called Local Harvest six eggs are probably twelve dollars even though Angela told me they have a mice problem the mice chew holes through the food containers and they still sell the food

so I shop at Ruler and oh look they are out of bananas too

the last time I was here the man in front of me bought a banana one banana he gave the cashier a quarter and the cashier gave him a dime back *one banana* the cashier said *I've never seen anyone buy one banana* I have never seen a Ruler cashier so happy so amused

the apples and oranges seem to look at me
I ask them what is happening
am I an apple am I an orange
well no the orange replies

I feel a warm hand wrap itself around my neck I look at the hand
and then my at body it has a tag it is
one color like the apples are one color like the oranges I weigh
an amount that amount is a value

you are yellow banana fifteen cents

halloween

the helicopters woke me up
last night they were looking
for the gunmen who fled their crime
on razor scooters
in the morning the reporters waited
by the police tape
for something
in the evening I saw
what they were waiting for
on my phone
where I can also look to see
if my roommates paid me back
for electricity
the killing was only two blocks away
but everyone's world is so different
people are so different from each other
we want different things
I almost don't notice
the lights go out on the train
when I was at theatre camp
one kid told everyone his brother got shot
the night before to get attention
it didn't happen and we all knew it
but every day is a threat the world might change
not into a different world but into the world
of someone else

it took me a while to see that
everyone else got off the train
except for me and a man
in all black
holding realistic angel wings

pain

I think this girl at work
doesn't like me
because I'm not sure about my pain
I want other people to tell me
how much pain I'm in
I see how that could be annoying

I record myself talking to kids
to see if I sound nice
sometimes I can tell
that the kids want to
cause me a bit of pain
and sometimes they ask me
if Nordstrom is where you go
when you die
because they don't really know
what happens with your body
if people keep using it
or not

Ellie taught me
how to draw a person
I need to focus on the light
and get an impression
of what's going on
I guess you would do
the same for an object

the girl wants me to have a clear
problem but I can't
experience pain in service
to a concept
it's hard for me to tell
if or why I feel pain
because it doesn't seem
contingent on anything

I was telling my uncle
about the acting training I did
how it was mostly just learning how
to get out of a chair
he asked if that seemed helpful
and I said I think it's always useful
to know where your body is

cascade mausoleum

we visit the mausoleum of a living man
nothing marks the tombs inside except light
stained with men   bowing to Jesus
the top floor is an outdoor platform
it symbolizes afterlife
Where the architects wrote *one is gifted*
glorious views   *otherwise hidden*
we lie on top of it and see
the landscape of graves below us

I think there may be a person with a body
inside me
we point at different headstones
looking for her name
Edith   *Luella*
        Gertrude   *June*
a Black name is often registered
as little more than an encounter with power

I could say I understand why
a person would spend millions of dollars
building a tall placc to rcst in
but I don't
we watch the sky thicken
until there is no air only earth it is mostly
like me silent

we were promised a sunrise

at the most easterly point
of North America
there is a cliff

in Newfoundland called Cape Spear
a battleground where
those who kept the light fought

my friend and I arrived
at 5:30 and alone
which means that day

in November we saw the most
time or light
but can time unblend itself

from light there wasn't a sunrise just
gray
then brighter gray

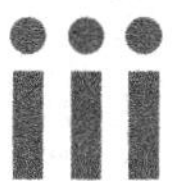

petrification

Fanon thought of petrification as a way to cope
with constant surveillance
stillness can be the body's attempt
to preserve its freedom
by never letting it enter a reality
in which its freedom
is being taken away

I went to see a play about slavery
the acting was stylized and dishonest
it seemed like the director
wanted everything to be funny
at the end of the show
the main character exposed her breast
to the audience
this was supposed to demonstrate
the new sense of ownership she felt over her body
after years of nursing white children
a few people laughed

in my dreams my dad is cheating on my mom

I ask my mom if they're real she says *I wish*
me and my mom don't have rich fantasy lives we have ambition
she wants to be press secretary of the United States
and my father is White so I have stood

at the foot of his mother's grave
in a cemetery of other graves
that all belong to White bodies

how powerful how dense and naked how inaccurate
my father's father says
you can be buried here too
if you like

there is no neutral

symmetrical sexual relationship
or exchange undistorted
by power
pleasure is like power
so I want it
and it makes me feel uncomfortable
A worries that I disconnect
during intimacy
so he asks me a lot of questions
do you want something different
sometimes I imagine
I'm in the captain's room
on a pirate ship
I can feel the waves
it's really fun
do you want something different
I usually say I'm not sure
but sometimes
I say no
do you want something different
I ask questions
to keep a conversation going
but A has a sincere curiosity about him
like a kid
in *The Book of Martha*
when Martha saw God

she was surprised God wasn't white
and her surprise surprised her
she said *I just thought*
I had already broken
out of the mental cage
I was born and raised in
—a human God, a white God, a male God
I do think of sex
as way of expressing closeness
I am afraid
of the unintended damage
that the dreams might do
Martha said to God
when she looked at God
and saw herself
because that's when she realized
God was a thing she created
do you want something different
we touch hands
in the morning

near north riverfront

I guess the state
put a halfway house
by the river
between an asphalt company
and the floodwall
I've walked past it before
but I didn't know
what it was
there are no signs
indicating a home
or anything
but my boyfriend
drove a cab
and picked someone up
who asked to go there
as quickly as possible
he explained that
he had to be home
by 8pm or else
he could be sent
back to prison

a block away
from the house
a group of eccentrics
burn down a wicker man

the fire is choreographed
so one arm falls
into the flames
then the other
before it all
becomes one thing
without parts

it's the biggest fire
I've ever seen
it reaches for us
the people watching

petrification

petrification is a certain numbness
the delirious disbelief
in which time is lived over and over again
it manifests physically as a stillness
that extends across a face
until it tenses into the expression
of a branch under a streetlight

Mr. Death is punishing me
because I didn't do my daily watercolor
Planetwalker said he was thinking
when he was walking through Colorado
and a policeman stopped him
and held a gun to his head

I wish I could stop performing freedom
it seems to benefit the audience more than me

nature

I like when outside and inside are indistinguishable
when I can't name the difference between nature and my house
in my tent I can see the stars and the palm trees in the morning

and the sunset is like desire and pleasure and A whispering *please*
in my ear sometimes I'm nature and I don't think it's bad
to be something other than human

I like to perform the role of human specimen
it's the only acting job in St. Louis that really pays
for $30 an hour you can pretend to have a health problem

and a not yet doctor will pretend to treat you
yesterday I decided to have hypertrophic cardiomyopathy
tomorrow I'll have a sprained ankle

when work is over I don't have a body anymore
there is no choosing what is happening
what is not happening

being in a relationship

I have been home for too long
at night I pretend to be my dog
until I want to look in the mirror
or check my friends' locations
one is in Miami Beach
we lived together a year ago
now she says
that's when she was most depressed
she has a lot of other friends
but I want her to think I'm special
my ex thinks so
and he does transcendental meditation
let's take your pacifier out
my boyfriend's brother's wife
says to my boyfriend's brother's baby
I don't think you need it
it's hard for me to take things
even when offered
but easy to do what someone says
the most popular question
on Quora today:
what does spending all this time
with someone else do to me
the most popular answer:
there is a lot of life
next to this one

real sounds

Arman saw a man on the street
          who he recognized
but he couldn't remember his name
          he remembered his first name
ends in J and it's not AJ or CJ
          once he told him a story
about when he was mugged
          the muggers told him to kneel
in front of the train tracks
          they told him he would die that night
something clicked and he decided to run
          and they did not kill him

I thought about what I would do
          and I'm worried I wouldn't
have run and might have died because of it
          I have to remember that it is important to run
even if nothing bad is going to happen
          and even if it seems safer to not run

when people die they escape their bodies
          which feels amazing
my boyfriend who briefly died
          didn't escape
his body so he continued
          living before he died
he bought a house and he didn't have a job

so he spent most days cleaning it
and doing projects to make it nicer
he has a difficult relationship with his parents
so he never asked them for money
but after he died he asked them to pay
for central AC for his house and they did

David's theory about taking prescription medication
for depression is that it is okay
because the world we are dealing with is artificial
and unnatural it is good
to counteract a fake world with the drugs
that it produces to make it more livable
my mom doesn't think I need medication
but she supports me trying new things

at my grandfather's funeral
the family was asked to drop roses
on top of his casket once it was deep
in the ground when the roses hit
the casket they made a terrible sound
it was like a scratch but not really
I don't know how to describe it
I wish he was buried in a wooden casket
so the roses would make a soft thump instead

my family spent a lot on the funeral programs
          and saved on the casket
the mahogany casket would have been expensive
          but words and pictures are not more important
than real sounds

petrification

i logged into a vigil
for a man who wasn't dead yet
he was executed an hour into the Zoom call

stillness isn't always still sometimes it's living
in the abyss
between nothingness and infinity

in *Slavers Throwing Overboard the Dead and Dying*

Turner breaks the water's surface with chained feet

open hands I look down at my still imagined body

the most difficult surface of water to represent is smooth

water without any visible rupture

the difficulty is reflection

if the surface is drawn without a reflection

the water looks like marble impenetrable

if it is drawn with leaves or a face the water becomes morbidly clear and endless

in an exhibition of his work called *The Sun Is God* there are no bodies

sometimes it's hard for me to tell if he painted water

or a field or a deer or the sky

in a cave where something once happened

—after performing
in an Afrofuturist rendition
of *A Midsummer Night's Dream*
in front of a mansion owned
by a man who killed a slave
I saw a color almost like black
when I was close enough
to touch it I could not see
my love's eyes just the holes
they sat in I realized then I don't
want to go inside black but I do
want the gray world black
creates those ambivalent holes
in his eyes are an area of hope

greenwood district

I tried to pull apart history
but when it opened it emptied
into a branch
and then another branch

I used to think
my people laughed in breath
fields of language

but breath is the space
between museums
and language is
the new chains inside them
artificially rusted to seem as if
they held a person

I won't stain this page
with what grows out
of the mud like teeth

but the light
the light stains me

Notes

In "perfoming," Portland Place refers to a wealthy micro-neighborhood in St. Louis where Mark and Patricia McCloskey live. During the George Floyd protests, they famously stood on their porch pointing guns at protestors.

In "mastery," the anonymous blogger quotes from Frank B. Wilderson's article "Afro-Pessimism and the End of Redemption."

"broken lyre" uses W. H. Auden's line "For poetry makes nothing happen: it survives" from "In Memory of W. B. Yeats."

"cascade mausoleum" refers to a mausoleum, currently unoccupied, in Bellefontaine Cemetery in St. Louis built for an anonymous wealthy person. The person gave the architect an open budget.

"petrification" quotes *Whither Fanon? Studies in the Blackness of Being*, by David Marriott. Planetwalker is a man named Dr. John Francis who walked for twenty-two years. He also kept a vow of silence for seventeen years.

"there is no neutral" quotes Jared Sexton's article "There Is No Interracial Sexual Relationship."

"in *Slavers Throwing Overboard the Dead and Dying"* is in response to a painting by J. M. W. Turner.

"greenwood district" references a historic freedom colony in Tulsa, Oklahoma.

Acknowledgments

Thank you to my family and friends, Kenyatta, Craig, Alijah, Angela, and Arman

Thank you to my teachers, Mary Jo Bang, Catherine Barnett, Regan Good, Miranda Field, and Carl Phillips

Thank you to my poet friends, David Ehmcke, Syd Westley, Carlota Gamboa, Abbey Frederick, Temperance Aghamohammadi, Safa Khatib, and Kathryn Hargett-Hsu

Thank you to Craig Morgan Teicher for seeing *Song of Gray* and selecting it to be published

Thank you to Ellie for making the cover and for friendship

Thank you to the publications in which some of these poems first appeared: *Poetry, Conduit*, *The Bennington Review*, *poets.org*, *The Journal*, *Common Place Poetics*, *Homophonic Sound Club*, and *Tyger Quarterly*

And thank you to The Song Cave for publishing several of these poems in a chapbook, *empathy*

THE COLORADO PRIZE FOR POETRY

Strike Anywhere,
by Dean Young
selected by Charles Simic, 1995

Summer Mystagogia,
by Bruce Beasley
selected by Charles Wright, 1996

The Thicket Daybreak,
by Catherine Webster
selected by Jane Miller, 1997

Palma Cathedral,
by Michael White
selected by Mark Strand, 1998

Popular Music,
by Stephen Burt
selected by Jorie Graham, 1999

Design,
by Sally Keith
selected by Allen Grossman, 2000

A Summer Evening,
by Geoffrey Nutter
selected by Jorie Graham, 2001

Chemical Wedding,
by Robyn Ewing
selected by Fanny Howe, 2002

Goldbeater's Skin,
by G. C. Waldrep
selected by Donald Revell, 2003

Whethering,
by Rusty Morrison
selected by Forrest Gander, 2004

Frayed escort,
by Karen Garthe
selected by Cal Bedient, 2005

Carrier Wave,
by Jaswinder Bolina
selected by Lyn Hejinian, 2006

Brenda Is in the Room and Other Poems,
by Craig Morgan Teicher
selected by Paul Hoover, 2007

One Sun Storm,
by Endi Bogue Hartigan
selected by Martha Ronk, 2008

The Lesser Fields,
by Rob Schlegel
selected by James Longenbach, 2009

Annulments,
by Zach Savich
selected by Donald Revell, 2010

Scared Text,
by Eric Baus
selected by Cole Swensen, 2011

Family System,
by Jack Christian
selected by Elizabeth Willis, 2012

Intimacy,
by Catherine Imbriglio
selected by Stephen Burt, 2013

Supplice,
by T. Zachary Cotler
selected by Claudia Keelan, 2014

The Business,
by Stephanie Lenox
selected by Laura Kasischke, 2015

Exit Theater,
by Mike Lala
selected by Tyrone Williams, 2016

Instead of Dying,
by Lauren Haldeman
selected by Susan Howe, 2017

The Owl Was a Baker's Daughter,
by Gillian Cummings
selected by John Yau, 2018

Magnifier,
by Brandon Krieg
selected by Kazim Ali, 2019

Night Burial,
by Kate Bolton Bonnici
selected by Kiki Petrosino, 2020

Study of the Raft,
by Leonora Simonovis
selected by Sherwin Bitsui, 2021

Human Is to Wander,
by Adrian Lürssen
selected by Gillian Conoley, 2022

Mountain Amnesia,
by Gale Marie Thompson
selected by Felicia Zamora, 2023

The Other Altar,
by Nicholas Gulig
selected by Brenda Shaughnessy, 2024

Song of Gray,
by Asha Futterman
selected by Craig Morgan Teicher, 2025

This book is set in Garamond ATF
and Twentieth Century MT Condensed
by The Center for Literary Publishing
at Colorado State University.

Copyediting by Autumn Koors-Foltz.
Proofreading by Sarah Stambaugh.
Book design and typesetting by Josephine Gawtry.
Cover art by Ellie Roussos.
Cover design by Stephanie G'Schwind.
Printing by Books International.